I Need You to Know...
#YouMatter

Positive Affirmations from A-Z

By: Lora McClain-Muhammad

Illustrated By: Bieunkah Anwojue & Asia Lewis-Ross

This Book Belongs to:

Dedication

To my daughter Che'la and
Lovey baby Eden Estelle, to my
daughters I've been blessed
with Paytyn, Paysiah and Rilee.
To all little children,
I Need You to Know...
#YOUMATTER!

xoxo,
Lori

I NEED YOU TO KNOW YOU ARE...

Beautiful

and

Brave

I NEED YOU TO KNOW YOU ARE...

Delightful and Dynamic

I NEED YOU TO KNOW YOU CAN BE AN...

I NEED YOU TO KNOW YOU ARE...

FIERCE

I NEED YOU TO KNOW YOU ARE...

Graceful

and

Gallant

FEATURING GAVIN!

HONOR GRAD

I NEED YOU TO KNOW YOU ARE...
Joyful and Jubilant

I NEED YOU TO KNOW YOU ARE...

Kingly

I NEED YOU TO KNOW #YouMatter...

Young Queen,
you are **MARVELOUS** and
wonderfully made!
Walk in your **MAGIC!**

I NEED YOU TO KNOW #YouMatter...

Young King,
Many have come before you and blazed a trail of **MAGNIFICENCE!** Your voice will be heard by the Masses! Now go and be great, your **MAJESTY!**

I NEED YOU TO KNOW YOU ARE...

One of a Kind

and

Outstanding

I NEED YOU TO KNOW YOU ARE...

Phenomenal and **Powerful**

I NEED YOU TO KNOW YOU ARE...

Spirited and Strong

I NEED YOU TO KNOW YOU ARE...

Valued

ISBN 978-1-7367108-0-7